Summary

Twenty-first century criminals increasingly rely on the Internet and advanced technologies to further their criminal operations. These criminals can easily leverage the Internet to carry out traditional crimes such as distributing illicit drugs and sex trafficking. In addition, they exploit the digital world to facilitate crimes that are often technology driven, including identity theft, payment card fraud, and intellectual property theft. Cybercrimes have economic, public health, and national security implications, among others. For over three decades, Congress has been concerned about cybercrime and its related threats. Today, these concerns often arise among a larger discussion surrounding the federal government's role in ensuring U.S. cyber security.

Conceptualizing cybercrime involves a number of key elements and questions that include *where* do the criminal acts exist in the real and digital worlds (and what technologies are involved in carrying out the crimes), *why* are malicious activities initiated, and *who* is involved in carrying out the malicious acts?

- One way of viewing cybercrimes is that they may be digital versions of traditional, real world offenses. They could be considered traditional, or "real world," crimes if not for the incorporated element of virtual or cyberspace. In some instances, however, it may seem that law enforcement struggles to keep up with developments in the virtual world, which transform routine activities once driven by paper records in the real world. As a result, criminals are often prosecuted using laws intended to combat crimes in the real world.

- The distinction between cybercrime and other malicious acts in the virtual realm is the actor's motivation. Cyber criminals can exhibit a wide range of self interests, deriving profit, notoriety, and/or gratification from activities such as hacking, cyber stalking, and online child pornography. Without knowing the criminal intent or motivation, however, some activities of cyber criminals and other malicious actors may appear on the surface to be similar, causing confusion as to whether a particular action should be categorized as cyber*crime* or not. When referring to cybercrime incidents, terms such as cyber attack, cyber espionage, and cyber war are often loosely applied, and they may obscure the motives of the actors involved.

- Criminal attribution is a key delineating factor between cybercrime and other cyber threats. When investigating a given threat, law enforcement is challenged with tracing the action to its source and determining whether the actor is a criminal or whether the actor may be a terrorist or state actor posing a potentially greater national security threat. This is highlighted by examining the online collective known as *Anonymous*. Some refer to Anonymous as a group of online activists, others see the collective as a group of criminal actors, and still others have likened it to online insurgents.

The U.S. government does not appear to have an official definition of cybercrime that distinguishes it from crimes committed in what is considered the real world. Similarly, there is not a definition of cybercrime that distinguishes it from other forms of cyber threats, and the term is often used interchangeably with other Internet- or technology-linked malicious acts. Federal law enforcement agencies often define cybercrime based on their jurisdiction and the crimes they are charged with investigating. And, just as there is no overarching definition for cybercrime, there is no single agency that has been designated as the lead investigative agency for combating cybercrime.

Congress may question whether it is necessary to have a clear definition of what constitutes cybercrime and what delineates it from other real world and cyber threats. On one hand, if the purpose of defining cybercrime is for investigating and prosecuting any of the various crimes under the broader cybercrime umbrella, it may be less critical to create a definition of the umbrella term and more imperative to clearly define which specific activities constitute crimes— regardless of whether they are considered real world crimes or cybercrimes. On the other hand, a distinction between cybercrime and other malicious activities may be beneficial for creating specific policies on combating the ever-expanding range of cyber threats. If government agencies and private sector businesses design strategies and missions around combating cybercrime, it may be useful to communicate a clear definition of cybercrime to those individuals who may be involved in carrying out the strategies.

The United States does not have a national strategy exclusively focused on combating cybercrime. Rather, there are other, broader strategies that have cybercrime components (a selection of which are presented in the **Appendix**). Policymakers may question whether there should be a distinct strategy for combating cybercrime or whether efforts to control these crimes are best addressed through more wide-ranging strategies such as those targeting cyber security or transnational organized crime. Congress may also question whether these broader strategies provide specific cybercrime-related objectives and clear means to achieve these goals.

Comprehensive data on cybercrime incidents and their impact are not available, and without exact numbers on the current scope and prevalence of cybercrime, it is difficult to evaluate the magnitude of the threats posed by cyber criminals. There are a number of issues that have prevented the accurate measurement and tracking of cybercrime. For one, the lack of a clear sense of what constitutes cybercrime presents a barrier to tracking inclusive cybercrime data. Additionally, much of the available data on cybercrime is self-reported, and individuals or organizations may not realize a cybercrime has taken place or may elect—for a host of reasons— not to report it. Policymakers may debate whether to direct a thorough evaluation of the threats posed by cyber criminals.

Contents

Appendixes

Contacts

Background

Twenty-first century criminals increasingly rely on the Internet and advanced technologies to further their criminal operations. According to Europol's 2011 Organized Crime Threat Assessment, "Internet technology has now emerged as a key facilitator for the vast majority of offline organised crime activity."[1] For instance, criminals can easily leverage the Internet to carry out traditional crimes such as distributing illicit drugs and sex trafficking. In addition, they exploit the digital world to facilitate crimes that are often technology driven, including identity theft, payment card fraud, and intellectual property theft. The Federal Bureau of Investigation (FBI) considers high-tech crimes to be the most significant crimes confronting the United States.[2] Policymakers have shown an increasing interest in ensuring the federal government has the tools and capabilities to combat modern day crime—particularly those with cyber components—while safeguarding privacy rights.[3]

Today's cyber criminals "have evolved their practices to make their crimes more profitable.... [T]hey choose specialties, master their skills, create networks of colleagues, and organize their crimes."[4] These criminals can victimize individuals and organizations alike. They are motivated by self interest and profit. One estimate has placed the annual cost of cybercrime to adults in 24 countries across the globe at $388 billion.[5] In addition to the economic impact, cybercrimes can have public health and national security consequences, among others.

U.S. officials face the challenging task of identifying the perpetrators of malicious cyber incidents in which victim and criminal can be far removed from one another. The person or persons behind an incident can range from lone actors to expansive criminal networks or even nation states. This challenge of actor attribution is further compounded by the anonymity afforded by the digital realm. It can sometimes be difficult to determine the actor's motivation—is the criminal driven by greed or glory in the form of recognition among fellow criminals in the cyber world, or does the criminal have broader ideological motives? Finding the answers to these questions is key to distinguishing between cybercrimes and other cyber threats such as cyber attacks, cyber espionage, and cyber warfare. Relevant distinctions exist between these various malicious

---

[1] Europol, *EU Organized Threat Assessment: OCTA 2011*, File No. 2530-274, April 28, 2011, p. 6, http://www.europol.europa.eu/publications/European_Organised_Crime_Threat_Assessment_%28OCTA%29/OCTA_2011.pdf.

[2] Steven R. Chabinsky, Deputy Assistant Director, Cyber Division, Federal Bureau of Investigation, GovSec/FOSE Conference, Washington, DC, http://www.fbi.gov/news/speeches/the-cyber-threat-whos-doing-what-to-whom. Hereafter: Chabinsky, GovSec/FOSE Conference.

[3] See, for example, U.S. Congress, Senate Committee on the Judiciary, Subcommittee on Crime and Drugs, *Cybersecurity: Evaluating the Administration's Proposals*, 112th Cong., 1st sess., June 21, 2011 as well as U.S. Congress, House Committee on the Judiciary, Subcommittee on Intellectual Property, Competition and the Internet, *Cybersecurity: Innovative Solutions to Challenging Problems*, 112th Cong., 1st sess., May 25, 2011.

[4] Chabinsky, GovSec/FOSE Conference.

[5] Norton, Symantec Corporation, "Norton Study Calculates Cost of Global Cybercrime: $114 Billion Annually," press release, September 7, 2011, http://www.symantec.com/about/news/release/article.jsp?prid=20110907_02. See also Norton, Symantec Corporation, *Cybercrime Report 2011*, http://www.symantec.com/content/en/us/home_homeoffice/html/cybercrimereport/. This $388 billion includes $114 billion in direct financial losses (amount stolen by cybercriminals and amount spent on resolving the cyber threats) as well as more than $274 billion in victim valued time lost to cybercrime.

---

activities in the cyber domain just as lines have been drawn between the their real world counterparts.

For over three decades, Congress has been concerned about cybercrime and its related threats.[6] Today, these concerns often arise among a larger discussion surrounding the federal government's role in ensuring cyber security.[7] This report discusses the concept of cybercrime and related cyber threats such as cyber espionage and cyber warfare. While it touches on these related threats, this report only does so in the context of framing the discussion of cybercrime.[8] It questions whether—and under what circumstances—clear distinctions between the various threats should be delineated. The report also outlines how current federal strategies may address cybercrime. It raises issues surrounding the measurement and tracking of cybercrime. Throughout, it discusses whether a clearer understanding of what constitutes cybercrime as well as its prevalence and harm could better equip policymakers to debate the sufficiency of federal law enforcement resources available to counter cybercrime and to conduct oversight in this arena.

Conceptualizing Cybercrime

A singular, agreed-upon definition of cybercrime does not exist. Various definitions have been offered by industry experts and scholars, and several have been formulated within the federal government. Definitions have varied in their levels of specificity and breadth. For instance, one of the largest computer security companies, Symantec Corporation, defines cybercrime as "any crime that is committed using a computer or network, or hardware device."[9] Irrespective of the definition, conceptualizing cybercrime involves a number of key elements and questions, including *where* do the criminal acts exist in the real and digital worlds (and what technologies are involved), *why* are malicious activities initiated, and *who* is involved in carrying out the malicious acts? In the sections below, the questions of where, why, and who are discussed as they relate to cybercrime. This is followed by a discussion of government definitions of cybercrime and a debate on whether or when a common definition of cybercrime may be useful.

Where: Location of Criminal Activities, Actors, and Victims

The notion of location as it relates to cybercrime involves both the physical and digital domains. The relatively clear borders and locations within the physical world, however, are not replicated in the virtual realm. Of course, some distinct boundaries separate the physical and the cyber worlds; keyboard, mouse, screen, and password can all mediate between these physical and virtual realms.[10] Within cyberspace, however, the notion of a border is much more nebulous. This

---

[6] The original version of the Computer Fraud and Abuse Act was passed as part of the Comprehensive Crime Control Act of 1984 (P.L. 98-473). Prior to this, hearings were held over several Congresses. For more information, see CRS Report 97-1025, *Cybercrime: An Overview of the Federal Computer Fraud and Abuse Statute and Related Federal Criminal Laws*, by Charles Doyle.

[7] For a list of hearings and cybersecurity legislation under consideration in the 112th Congress, among other things, see CRS Report R42507, *Cybersecurity: Authoritative Reports and Resources*, by Rita Tehan.

[8] For more information on cyberwarfare and other cybersecurity issues, see CRS Report RL31787, *Information Operations, Cyberwarfare, and Cybersecurity: Capabilities and Related Policy Issues*, by Catherine A. Theohary.

[9] Symantec Corporation, *What is Cybercrime?*, http://us norton.com/cybercrime/definition.jsp.

[10] David R. Johnson and David Post, "Law and Borders - The Rise of Law in Cyberspace," *Stanford Law Review*, vol. 48 (May 1996), p. 1379.

---

is, in part, because the same geographic borders that exist in the real world do not exist in the cyber world.[11]

Even without distinct borders, the digital world is linked to the physical world—as is crime involving the digital world. Take, for instance, point-of-sale skimming. This high-tech financial fraud involves placing a device over (or sometimes replacing) an existing card slot on a credit card reader or ATM. The device "relies on sophisticated data-reading electronics to copy the magnetic stripe information from [the] credit card or debit card. It can capture both [the] credit card number and [the] PIN."[12] Fraudsters can then retrieve the stolen information by physically collecting the skimming device or by programming the device to broadcast the data to thieves over a network.

Researchers have proposed that some cybercrimes may require more technological expertise or heavier use of digital technologies to perpetrate than others.[13] For example, phishing,[14] identity theft, and distributed denial of service (DDoS)[15] attacks necessitate a greater understanding of computing and digital technologies than others, such as cyber stalking and online child pornography, that can be thought of as "point and click" crimes. Those crimes requiring more technological expertise may also be more firmly rooted in the virtual world than others. Regardless, the cyber component may delineate them from traditional crimes. Computers and other advanced technologies may be components of cybercrime through a variety of roles:

- in some cybercrimes, computers themselves—or data contained therein—are the victims or targets of crime;

- in other instances, computers or other digital technologies are used as tools for carrying out crimes (victimizing individuals, organizations, or government); and

- technological devices may serve as repositories for evidence of a cybercrime.[16]

All of these issues underscore the salience of location in any conceptualization of cybercrime.

---

[11] David R. Johnson and David Post, "Law and Borders - The Rise of Law in Cyberspace," *Stanford Law Review*, vol. 48 (May 1996), p. 1370.

[12] Robert Vamosi, "Keep Your Credit Cards Safe From Skimmers," *PC World*, December 8, 2010.

[13] Sarah Gordon and Richard Ford, "On the definition and classification of cybercrime," *Journal of Computer Virology*, vol. 2 (July 2006), pp. 15 – 19.

[14] Phishing "is a technique used to gain personal information for purposes of identity theft, using fraudulent e-mail messages that appear to come from legitimate businesses. These authentic-looking messages are designed to fool recipients into divulging personal data such as account numbers and passwords, credit card numbers and Social Security numbers," Computerworld, January 19, 2004, http://www.computerworld.com/s/article/89096/Phishing.

[15] A denial-of-service attack attempts to prevent legitimate users from accessing a resource – in this case a network or website. This is most commonly done by "flooding" a network with information and overloading the server with so many requests for information that it cannot process other, legitimate requests. A distributed denial-of-service (DDoS) attack utilizes other computers—often from unwitting individuals—to assist in flooding a network. For more information, see the U.S. Computer Emergency Readiness Team, http://www.us-cert.gov/cas/tips/ST04-015 html.

[16] According to the Homeland Security Newswire, "[t]he ubiquity of this [electronic] technology [such as cell phones and computer files] has often provided investigators with an electronic trail that gives prosecutors concrete analytical evidence for nearly every crime." "An Electronic Trail for Every Crime," *Homeland Security Newswire*, April 19, 2011, http://homelandsecuritynewswire.com/electronic-trail-every-crime.

Technology: Cyber vs. Real World Crime

Perhaps one way of viewing cybercrimes is that they are digital versions of traditional offenses.[17] It appears that many cybercrimes could be considered traditional, or real world, crimes if not for the incorporated element of virtual or cyberspace. Indeed, many of these so-called cybercrimes can be easily likened to traditional crimes. For instance, identity theft can occur in both physical and cyber arenas. While these crimes may occur through differing mechanisms, in both circumstances the criminal intent (profit) and outcome (stolen personally identifiable information) are the same.

- In the real world, a criminal can steal a victim's wallet or mail including documents containing personally identifiable information. In April 2011, two men were sentenced for leading a criminal enterprise that stole credit and debit cards from mailboxes in affluent neighborhoods in South Florida. The thieves then used the cards to make large purchases and cash withdrawals from the cards, costing victims $786,000.[18] In another case, from September 2010, the leaders of a mail theft and identity theft ring were sentenced for stealing mail from mailboxes in more than 50 residences and law firms in Washington, D.C. The thieves took checks and documents containing personally identifiable information (PII) to cash forged checks at local banks.[19]

- In the cyber world, a computer hacker can easily steal this same PII— electronically rather than physically. In November 2011, a member of a Romanian criminal organization was sentenced for his role in a large scale bank fraud and identity theft scam. Dan Petri and co-conspirators installed high-tech skimming devices on bank automated teller machines (ATMs). These devices illegally captured victims' bank account information and PINs, which the fraudsters used to create duplicate cards and withdraw large sums of money, ultimately scamming victims out of more than $276,800.[20] In another case, two defendants were sentenced in July 2010 for using peer-to-peer (P2P) software to search file sharing networks, stealing victims' account information and passwords. The defendants used this information to access victims' bank accounts and transfer funds to prepaid credit cards in the defendants' names.[21]

In some instances, it may seem that law enforcement struggles to keep up with developments in the virtual world, which transform routine activities once driven by paper records in the real world. As a result, criminals are often prosecuted using laws intended to combat crimes in the real

---

[17] Susan Brenner, "Thoughts, Witches and Crimes," *CYB3RCRIM3: Observations on Technology, Law, and Lawlessness*, May 6, 2009, http://cyb3rcrim3.blogspot.com/2009/05/thoughts-witches-and-crimes.html.

[18] U.S. Department of Justice, "Two Wellington Men Sentenced in Mail and Aggravated Identity Theft Ring," press release, April 26, 2011, http://www.justice.gov/usao/fls/PressReleases/110426-03.html; Wayne K. Roustan, "Two Plead Guilty to ID Theft That Cost Victims $786,000: They Admit Stealing Credit and Debit Cards from Mailboxes," February 12, 2011.

[19] U.S. Department of Justice, "Leaders of Mail Theft and Identity Theft Ring Get Prison Terms - Took Mail From Residences, Law Firms," press release, September 23, 2010, http://www.justice.gov/usao/dc/news/2010/sep/10-250.pdf.

[20] U.S. Department of Justice, "Member Of Prolific Romanian "Skimming" Ring Sentenced To Five Years In Prison," press release, November 18, 2011, http://www.justice.gov/usao/waw/press/2011/nov/petri.html.

[21] U.S. Department of Justice, press release, July 9, 2010, http://www.justice.gov/usao/cas/press/cas10-0709-Girandola.pdf.

world. As Department of Justice (DOJ) officials have pointed out, federal laws to prosecute computer-related crimes are not necessarily as ample or broad as those used to confront their traditional counterparts.[22] For instance, computer fraud (18 U.S.C. §1030) is not currently considered a predicate offense for racketeering under the Racketeer Influenced Corrupt Organizations (RICO) Act—one of the primary tools used to prosecute organized crime.[23] As noted, organized criminals are increasingly using the Internet and other advanced technologies to carry out their operations. Yet, the range of crimes carried out by organized crime encompasses both traditional and cybercrimes. The Obama Administration has recommended revising RICO provisions (which can be applied to both criminal and civil cases) so that computer fraud would be considered a predicate offense.[24] Cyber criminal organizations have been targeted under civil RICO, citing predicate offenses such as wire fraud, bank fraud, and access device fraud.[25] It is unknown whether or how adding computer fraud to the list of predicate offenses would further these investigations and prosecutions.

- In March 2012, Microsoft Corporation and co-plaintiffs filed a civil complaint against 39 individuals involved with the computer network known as the Zeus botnet.[26] Microsoft had been granted court approval to seize 800 domains and several servers in Pennsylvania and Illinois that had been used to control the Zeus and SpyEye botnets.[27] Both Zeus and SpyEye would steal online banking information. They would then transfer funds to money mules, or U.S. residents with bank accounts, who would move the money out of the United States.

Borders and Cyberspace

Criminals operate in the cyber world partly to circumvent more conventional, established constructs such as international borders.[28] In the virtual realm, criminals can rely on relative anonymity and a rather seamless environment to conduct business. High-speed Internet communication has not only facilitated the growth of legitimate business, but it has bolstered criminals' abilities to operate in an environment where they can broaden their pool of potential targets and rapidly exploit their victims. Between December 2000 and December 2011, the estimated number of Internet users grew from almost 361 million to nearly 7 billion—an increase

---

[22] Statement for the Record of James A. Baker, Associate Deputy Attorney General, Department of Justice before the U.S. Congress, House Committee on the Judiciary, Subcommittee on Crime, Terrorism, and Homeland Security, *Cybersecurity: Innovative Solutions to Challenging Problems*, 112th Cong., May 25, 2011, http://judiciary house.gov/hearings/pdf/Baker05252011.pdf.

[23] For more information on RICO, see CRS Report 96-950, *RICO: A Brief Sketch*, by Charles Doyle. The predicate offenses for racketeering include a host of state and federal crimes listed in 18 U.S.C. §1961.

[24] The White House, *Law Enforcement Provisions Related to Computer Security*, May 12, 2011, p. 2, http://www.whitehouse.gov/omb/legislative_letters. Legislation (e.g., the Cyber Crime Protection Security Act, S. 2111) introduced in the 112th Congress would, among other things, make computer fraud and related crimes under 18 U.S.C. §1030 predicate offenses under RICO.

[25] "Microsoft Takes Down Dozens of Zeus, SpyEye Botnets," *Krebs on Security*, March 26, 2012. See also *Microsoft Corp., FS-ISAC, Inc., and National Automated Clearing House Association v. John Does 1-39*, (U.S. District Court, Eastern District of New York), http://www.zeuslegalnotice.com/images/Complaint_w_Appendices.pdf.

[26] Botnets are groups of computers that are remotely controlled by hackers. They have been infected by downloading malicious software and are used to carry out malicious activities on behalf of the hackers.

[27] *Microsoft Corp., FS-ISAC, Inc., and National Automated Clearing House Association v. John Does 1-39*, (U.S. District Court, Eastern District of New York), http://www.zeuslegalnotice.com/images/Complaint_w_Appendices.pdf.

[28] For more information on the issue of borders in cyberspace, see CRS Report R41927, *The Interplay of Borders, Turf, Cyberspace, and Jurisdiction: Issues Confronting U.S. Law Enforcement*, by Kristin M. Finklea.

---

of more than 528%.[29] Frauds and schemes that were once conducted face-to-face can now be carried out remotely from across the country or even across the world. Despite criminals exploiting virtual space, the criminal actor and the victim(s) are located in the real world—though often in different cities, states, or even countries. Similarly, the digital technologies used to facilitate these crimes, such as Internet servers and digital communication devices, are located in physical locations that may not coincide with the locations of the criminal actors or victims. As such, law enforcement faces not only technological but jurisdictional challenges in investigating and prosecuting cyber criminals.

Conceptualizing Cyberspace

In determining what constitutes cybercrime, it may be beneficial to outline what constitutes cyberspace. After determining what constitutes the cyber realm, then boundaries for permissible behavior—as it intersects with this space—can be outlined.

The National Security Presidential Directive 54/Homeland Security Presidential Directive 23 (NSPD-54/HSPD-23), defines cyberspace as "the interdependent network of information technology infrastructures, and includes the Internet, telecommunications networks, computer systems, and embedded processors and controllers in critical industries." In other words, cyberspace is the "virtual environment of information and interactions between people."[30] The U.S. Military has adopted a definition of cyberspace consistent with that laid out in NSPD-54/HSPD-23. A 2008 Deputy Secretary of Defense Memorandum defined cyberspace as "[a] global domain within the information environment consisting of the interdependent network of information technology infrastructures, including the Internet, telecommunications networks, computer systems, and embedded processors and controllers."[31] It is unknown whether federal law enforcement also utilizes the definition of cyberspace—as outlined in NSPD-54/HSPD-23— in its conceptualization of what constitutes cybercrime and for purposes of cybercrime investigations and prosecutions.

As noted by one expert, cyberspace "is not a fixed, predetermined reality operating according to principles and dynamics that cannot be controlled or altered by man. The cyberworld is a constructed world, a fabrication. Because it is a construct, cyberspace is mutable; much of it can be modified and transformed."[32] Criminal actors do not exist in cyberspace. Rather, they exist in the physical world and their actions traverse the real world as well as cyberspace, impacting victims in the real world. In this vein, criminals may rely upon cyberspace as a marketplace to help carry out malicious activities, but they—and their victims—remain in the physical world.

---

[29] Internet World Stats, *Internet Usage Statistics, The Internet Big Picture, World Internet Users and Population Stats*, http://www.internetworldstats.com/stats htm.

[30] National Security Agency, *Statement for the Record, Lieutenant General Keith Alexander, Commander, Joint Functional Component Command for Network Warfare*, Before the House Armed Services Committee, Terrorism, Unconventional Threats, and Capabilities Subcommittee, May 5, 2009, http://www.nsa.gov/public_info/ speeches_testimonies/5may09_dir.shtml.

[31] See Deputy Secretary of Defense Memorandum, Subject: *The Definition of Cyberspace*, May 12, 2008. Other defense documents have defined cyberspace as a warfighting domain, an operational domain, and a global commons. See, for example, the 2010 Quadrennial Defense Review.

[32] Susan W. Brenner, "Organized Cybercrime? How Cyberspace May Affect the Structure of Criminal Relationships," *North Carolina Journal of Law & Technology*, vol. 4, no. 1 (Fall), p. 37.

Why: Motivation

The distinction between cybercrime and other cyber-based malicious acts such as terrorism or state sponsored espionage is the actor's *motivation*. Cyber criminals can exhibit a wide range of self interests, deriving profit, notoriety, and/or gratification from activities such as hacking, cyber stalking, and online child pornography. As one FBI agent specializing in cybercrime has reportedly stated, "[h]acking into a company, whether it's to put information on the web for everyone to see or if you're going to make money, is still hacking, it's still a crime."[33] Without knowing the criminal intent or motivation, however, some activities of cyber criminals and other malicious actors may appear on the surface to be similar, causing confusion as to whether a particular action should be categorized as cyber*crime* or not. As noted in the National Strategy to Secure Cyberspace, "[t]he speed and anonymity of cyber attacks makes distinguishing among the actions of terrorists, criminals, and nation states difficult, a task which often occurs only after the fact, if at all."[34] This challenge of attribution is discussed in detail in the section "Who: Attribution."

The FBI has noted three primary categories of cyber threat actors:

> [1] organized crime groups that are primarily threatening the financial services sector, and they are expanding the scope of their attacks; [2] state sponsors—foreign governments that are interested in pilfering data, including intellectual property and research and development data from major manufacturers, government agencies, and defense contractors; and [3] increasingly there are terrorist groups who want to impact this country the same way they did on 9/11 by flying planes into buildings. They are seeking to use the network to challenge the United States by looking at critical infrastructure to disrupt or harm the viability of our way of life.[35]

Of these three categories outlined by the FBI, the first—organized crime groups—focuses on cybercrime. However, this category appears limited to those crimes that target the financial services sector. While the second category includes the theft of intellectual property and other activities that may be considered cybercrimes, this category is more roughly aligned with state-sponsored espionage. As such, the FBI's conceptualization of cybercrime surrounds the activities—primarily financial—of organized crime groups. This may exclude lone actors including hackers, stalkers, and online child predators. The FBI considers these malicious activities under the umbrella of cybercrime, as discussed in the "Government Definitions and Agency Focus" section of this report, but the classification noted above suggests that the FBI may prioritize investigation of criminal organizations engaging in cybercrime over lone actors.

While there is a clear distinction that organized crime groups are motivated by profit and terrorists are motivated by ideologies, the motivation of state sponsored cyber threat actors may be more difficult to categorize and determine. This may be in part because different state sponsored actors may have different motivations, as is implied by the FBI description of the range of state sponsored cyber threats. For instance, some actors targeting the intellectual property of

---

[33] Dominic Rushe, "FBI Fights Back Against Cybercrime," *The Guardian*, August 24, 2011, http://www.guardian.co.uk/technology/2011/aug/24/us-agency-fights-back-against-cybercrime.

[34] Department of Homeland Security, *National Strategy to Secure Cyberspace*, February 2003, p. viii, http://www.dhs.gov/xlibrary/assets/National_Cyberspace_Strategy.pdf.

[35] Federal Bureau of Investigation, *The Cyber Threat: Part 1: On the Front Lines With Shawn Henry*, March 27, 2012, http://www.fbi.gov/news/stories/2012/march/shawn-henry_032712/shawn-henry_032712.

manufacturers and corporations may aim to gain a competitive advantage for businesses based in a particular country. Others actors seeking data from government agencies and contractors may desire to utilize this information to undermine the integrity and security of a rival nation. This is the distinction between the theft of trade secrets and the theft of state secrets. Nonetheless, in some cases, state actors' actions look much like those of profit-driven criminals.

Blurring Lines Between Cybercrime and Related Threats

When referring to cybercrime incidents, terms such as cyber attack and cyber war are often loosely applied, and they may obscure the motives of the actors involved. Blurring of concepts occurs in other areas as well. The terms cyber espionage or exploitation and cyber attack are often used interchangeably, although they may refer to distinct sets of activities that are governed by different laws, regulations, or strategies. However, there are areas where these activities may overlap, causing confusion over the applicable governing structure. Experts have cautioned that overuse of the term cyber war or information warfare when referring to cybercrime may sensationalize certain cybercrimes that are threats to public security but not necessarily threats to national security.[36]

Organized Criminals in Cyberspace—A National Security Threat

Significant threats posed by cybercrime may be considered matters of national and economic security. For instance, the White House, through the Strategy to Combat Transnational Organized Crime (Strategy), has indicated that cybercrime "costs consumers billions of dollars annually, threatens sensitive corporate and government computer networks, and undermines worldwide confidence in the international financial system."[37] Criminal networks rely on cyber technologies to carry out sophisticated frauds costing individuals and businesses billions of dollars. The Strategy notes that over the course of one year, Central European cybercrime networks alone have defrauded U.S. persons and businesses of about 1 billion dollars.[38]

- In one recent case, more than 100 members of Romanian-based organized criminal groups have been arrested for their participation in a wire fraud scheme. Co-conspirators—from countries including Romania, Moldova, and the United States—would post items for sale on Internet auction and online websites. Individuals interested in purchasing these items were instructed to wire money to bank accounts that had been opened under fictitious names. The alleged fraudsters received the money (more than $10 million in reported profits), but the victims never received their purchased goods.[39]

- In another case, one network of hackers—from countries including Estonia, Russia, and Moldova—reportedly hacked the RBS WorldPay computer network.

---

[36] David L. Speer, "Redefining Borders: The Challenges of Cybercrime," *Crime, Law and Social Change*, vol. 34, no. 3 (October 2000), p. 260.

[37] The White House, *Strategy To Combat Transnational Organized Crime: Addressing Converging Threats to National Security*, July 2011, p. 7, http://www.whitehouse.gov/sites/default/files/microsites/2011-strategy-combat-transnational-organized-crime.pdf.

[38] Ibid., p. 7.

[39] U.S. Department of Justice, "Organized Romanian Criminal Groups Targeted by DOJ and Romanian Law Enforcement," press release, July 15, 2011, http://www.justice.gov/opa/pr/2011/July/11-crm-926.html.

These individuals allegedly defeated the encryption used by RBS WorldPay to protect customer information associated with the payroll card processing system. Using counterfeit payroll debit cards—cards that allow employees to withdraw their regular salaries from ATMs—the hackers and their associates withdrew more than $9.4 million from over 2,100 ATMs across at least 280 cities around the globe—including in the United States, Russia, Ukraine, Estonia, Italy, Hong Kong, Japan, and Canada. Notably, the over $9 million loss occurred in under 12 hours.[40]

Cyber Espionage—Profit vs. State Direction

Espionage conducted in cyberspace is in many ways akin to traditional forms of espionage, the unauthorized access to confidential information by an individual or government. Illicit exfiltration of networked information can be conducted for intelligence gathering purposes, financial gains, or a combination of the two. Cyber espionage—particularly that which targets trade secrets—can pose similar threats to national security. According to the Office of the National Counterintelligence Executive, "[f]oreign economic collection and industrial espionage against the United States represent significant and growing threats to the nation's prosperity and security."[41] Cyber espionage targeting trade secrets can be considered either distinct from, or a form of, cybercrime depending upon the actor and the actor's motivation. Economic[42] and industrial espionage[43] (or theft of trade secrets) financially burden U.S. companies that lose valuable intellectual property and incur costs in remediating the damage from the theft.

The use of technology for these purposes is nothing new; spying in cyberspace is a criminal activity as it is in other domains. However, the tools used to conduct cyber spying can be the same as those used to commit a host of disruptive or destructive acts that could range from online activism to criminal activity, and conceivably even an act of war.

---

[40] U.S. Department of Justice, "International Hacker Arraigned After Extradition," press release, August 6, 2010, http://www.justice.gov/usao/gan/press/2010/08-06-10.pdf.

[41] Office of the National Counterintelligence Executive, *Foreign Spies Stealing US Economic Secrets in Cyberspace: Report to Congress on Foreign Economic Collection and Industrial Espionage, 2009-2011*, October 2011, p. i.

[42] 18 U.S.C. §1831. Economic espionage is "(a) In General—Whoever, intending or knowing that the offense will benefit any foreign government, foreign instrumentality, or foreign agent, knowingly – (1) steals, or without authorization appropriates, takes, carries away, or conceals, or by fraud, artifice, or deception obtains a trade secret; (2) without authorization copies, duplicates, sketches, draws, photographs, downloads, uploads, alters, destroys, photocopies, replicates, transmits, delivers, sends, mails, communicates, or conveys a trade secret; (3) receives, buys, or possesses a trade secret, knowing the same to have been stolen or appropriated, obtained, or converted without authorization; (4) attempts to commit any offense described in any of paragraphs (1) through (3); or (5) conspires with one or more other persons to commit any offense described in any of paragraphs (1) through (3), and one or more of such persons do any act to effect the object of the conspiracy."

[43] 18 U.S.C. §1832. Theft of trade secrets is when an individual "knowingly – (1) steals, or without authorization appropriates, takes, carries away, or conceals, or by fraud, artifice, or deception obtains such information; (2) without authorization copies, duplicates, sketches, draws, photographs, downloads, uploads, alters, destroys, photocopies, replicates, transmits, delivers, sends, mails, communicates, or conveys such information; (3) receives, buys, or possesses such information, knowing the same to have been stolen or appropriated, obtained, or converted without authorization; (4) attempts to commit any offense described in paragraphs (1) through (3); or (5) conspires with one or more other persons to commit any offense described in paragraphs (1) through (3), and one or more of such persons do any act to effect the object of the conspiracy."

- Consider the reported hacking of computer systems used in the design of the U.S. military's multipurpose fighter jet, the Joint Strike Fighter.[44] In some ways, this represents a typical case of industrial espionage in which plans for a company's product are illegally obtained and replicated. However, as a military platform it is difficult to ascertain whether its computerized operating systems were hacked in order to understand and replicate them or to plant malicious software that could conduct military surveillance, or potentially disrupt or destroy the platform's ability to function. Complicating this is the lack of clear attribution for the perpetrators. Although the security breach appeared to have origins in China, without an understanding of whether it was sponsored by a foreign government or military, it is difficult to categorize whether the hacking was merely a criminal activity or part of what could be considered an economic espionage campaign.[45] For its part, officials from the People's Republic of China have denied responsibility, stating that all forms of computer hacking are illegal in China, and that the government has difficulty in controlling computer crime within its own borders.

Cyber Warfare

Three international incidents involving Estonia, Georgia, and Iran have influenced recent discussions of what distinguishes cyber warfare from related cyber threats. In 2007, a series of distributed denial of service (DDOS) attacks were launched on Estonian websites and networked services. Although it appeared that the attacks may have come from Russia, some of the IP addresses involved were traced to ethnic Russians living within Estonian borders.[46] Without a definition of what constitutes an "armed attack" in cyberspace and where territorial boundaries exist, and without attribution to a nation state, some considered the Estonian cyber attacks to be more of a cyber riot than a war. Some considered it the electronic equivalent to a real world sit-in, in that traffic to particular sites was analogously slowed down or blocked by organized citizens wishing to make a political statement or influence events. Others have likened it to a form of cyber terrorism, another term for which no consensus definition exists.[47] Ultimately, although various groups have claimed credit for the attacks, investigations led to only one conviction in an Estonian criminal court of an ethnic Russian student.

Soon after the Estonian incident, there was a series of strategic cyber attacks that disabled Georgian command and control systems in 2008. This coincided with a Russian military incursion across the Georgian border. As the cyber disruption occurred simultaneously with a kinetic event, some considered this to be a form of network warfare. Some questioned whether this disruption was an act of cyber warfare by the Russians or a separate cyber threat.

---

[44] First reported in The Wall Street Journal, Siobhan Gorban, August Cole, and Yochi Dreazen, *Computer Spies Breach Fighter Jet Program*, April 21, 2009.

[45] "Moonlight Maze" and "Titan Rain" are examples of cyber campaigns conducted against unclassified Department of Defense targets and directed by other governments. Probes may be used to test network defenses as well as to extract sensitive information, and may coincide with a country's interest in weakening U.S. command and control systems.

[46] For a country so wired that it is colloquially known as E-stonia, the attacks had such a crippling effect that Estonian government officials considered it a national security crisis. At the time, Estonia appealed to the Russian government for help under a Mutual Legal Assistance treaty, but was denied.

[47] For information on terrorist use of the Internet, see CRS Report R41674, *Terrorist Use of the Internet: Information Operations in Cyberspace*, by Catherine A. Theohary and John Rollins.

Investigations later determined that the attacks began with online Russian hacking forums, who distributed lists of Georgian internet sites as targets.

In July 2010, a malicious software worm called Stuxnet attacked the operations of nuclear centrifuges in Iran.[48] Some assumed that only a nation state or states would have the intelligence apparatus and testing beds necessary to develop and deploy this malware. In addition, as the worm was designed to target and destroy particular systems without any financial or intelligence gain, Stuxnet may be considered a form of cyber weaponry rather than a different form of cyber threat such as cyber espionage or cybercrime.

Who: Attribution

The preceding section suggests that blurry lines between various types of malicious activity in cyberspace may make it difficult for investigators to attribute an incident to a specific individual or organization. Criminal attribution is a key delineating factor between cybercrime and other cyber threats. When investigating a given threat, law enforcement is challenged with tracing the action to its source and determining whether the actor is a criminal or whether the actor may be a terrorist or state actor posing a potentially greater national security threat.

Take, for example, the July–September 2011 attacks on private companies primarily involved in the chemical industry. In what has been dubbed the "Nitro" attacks, hackers sent phony emails to members of Fortune 100 companies, businesses developing advanced materials for military vehicles, and companies developing manufacturing infrastructure for the chemical industry.[49] The emails contained attachments with a malicious Trojan[50] called PoisonIvy, which ultimately allowed hackers access to other computers in the company workgroup as well as to needed passwords. They could then navigate to the targeted intellectual property, copy the content, and upload the information to servers external to the compromised organization. Because the victimized companies were involved in the research, development, and manufacture of chemicals and advanced materials, it may have initially been unclear whether the attacker was a terrorist attempting to procure chemicals or a hacker seeking corporate secrets. According to Symantec, the purpose of the attacks was likely industrial espionage, and the attackers appear to have been seeking intellectual property, including design documents, formulas, and manufacturing processes, for competitive advantage. The source of the attack was identified as a computer system owned by an individual—dubbed Covert Grove—in China.[51]

Attribution continues to be a challenge in identifying both public security and national security threats. In the 2012 Worldwide Threat Assessment of the U.S. Intelligence Community, James

---

[48] See CRS Report R41524, *The Stuxnet Computer Worm: Harbinger of an Emerging Warfare Capability*, by Paul K. Kerr, John Rollins, and Catherine A. Theohary.

[49] Eric Chien and Gavin O'Gorman, *The Nitro Attacks: Stealing Secrets from the Chemical Industry*, Symantec Security Response, 2011, http://www.symantec.com/content/en/us/enterprise/media/security_response/whitepapers/ the_nitro_attacks.pdf.

[50] A Trojan is a type of malware. It is a type of software that, once activated, can damage the host and provide back doors for malicious users to access the computer system. For more information on the various types of malware, see Cisco, *What Is the Difference: Viruses, Worms, Trojans, and Bots?*, http://www.cisco.com/web/about/security/ intelligence/virus-worm-diffs html.

[51] Eric Chien and Gavin O'Gorman, *The Nitro Attacks: Stealing Secrets from the Chemical Industry*, Symantec Security Response, 2011, http://www.symantec.com/content/en/us/enterprise/media/security_response/whitepapers/ the_nitro_attacks.pdf.

Clapper, Director of National Intelligence, outlined cyber threats as the third most pressing threat to national security—behind terrorism and nuclear proliferation—and noted the challenges in cyber actor attribution. More specifically, he noted that

> [t]wo of our greatest strategic challenges regarding cyber threats are: (1) the difficulty of providing timely, actionable warning of cyber threats and incidents, such as identifying past or present security breaches, *definitively attributing them* [emphasis added], and accurately distinguishing between cyber espionage intrusions and potentially disruptive cyber attacks; and (2) the highly complex vulnerabilities associated with the IT supply chain for US networks.[52]

Attribution, however, may be more important for government and law enforcement than for private sector organizations. Law enforcement, through their investigations, may strive for attribution so that the actual perpetrator may be prosecuted. Industry organizations, however, may be less concerned and may focus more on damage control and prevention—regardless of the actor or his motivations.[53]

Case Study: Anonymous

The online collective known as "Anonymous" is a decentralized group operating in cyberspace. While scholars, theorists, law enforcement, and policymakers may not always agree on how to conceptualize or categorize the Anonymous entity, it is generally agreed that it operates with two broad tenets: (1) personal anonymity and (2) the free flow of information.[54] Anonymous is a loosely formed organization to the extent that it cannot be easily categorized. For instance, membership may be fluid; the Anonymous structure—or lack thereof—allows for participation in a single campaign or in a variety of protest activities. Further, members may have different interests and motivations for participation, and may use differing forms of tactics—both legal and illegal. As such, some refer to Anonymous as a group of online activists, others see the collective as a group of criminal actors, and still others have likened it to online insurgents.[55]

Anonymous came into the spotlight in 2008 with its first united act of "hacktivism"[56] to protest the Church of Scientology. The church reportedly attempted to pressure Internet websites to remove a leaked video of actor Tom Cruise endorsing Scientology—a video that had only been intended for church viewing.[57] In response, Anonymous members banded together to make distributed denial-of-service (DDoS) attacks, amongst other things (such as prank calling, hosting proprietary church documents online, and sending excessive faxes to waste paper and ink) against the church.[58] This online protest later transitioned to physical protest, with masked activists

---

[52] Office of the Director of National Intelligence, *Unclassified Statement for the Record on the Worldwide Threat Assessment of the US Intelligence Community for the Senate Select Committee on Intelligence*, January 31, 2012, p. 8.

[53] Office of the National Counterintelligence Executive, *Foreign Spies Stealing US Economic Secrets in Cyberspace: Report to Congress on Foreign Economic Collection and Industrial Espionage, 2009-2011*, October 2011, p. 1.

[54] From remarks by Gabriella Coleman, Professor, New York University, at The Brookings Institution, *Hacktivism, Vigilantism and Collective Action in a Digital Age*, November 9, 2011.

[55] From remarks by Paul Rosenzweig, Lecturer in Law, George Washington University, at The Brookings Institution, *Hacktivism, Vigilantism and Collective Action in a Digital Age*, November 9, 2011.

[56] Hacktivism is a term often used to refer to the use of computers and online networks to conduct politically or socially-motivated protest.

[57] E. Gabriella Coleman, "Anonymous: From the Lulz to Collective Action," *The New Everyday*, April 6, 2011.

[58] Ryan Singel, "War Breaks Out Between Hackers and Scientology—There Can Be Only One," *Wired: Threat Level*, (continued...)

gathering outside of Scientology compounds.[59] In another notable display of online hacktivism, Anonymous initiated DDoS attacks against PayPal, Mastercard, Amazon, and others in December 2010. This was in response to these companies pulling support and services for Wikileaks, which had publicly released a cache of diplomatic cables.[60]

The first instance of Anonymous hacking networks for the purpose of exposing data was against the security firm HBGary.[61] HBGary had reportedly uncovered the identities of Anonymous leaders and was planning to release this information to the FBI. Anonymous hacked into HBGary's servers and published the company's email online, exposing sensitive proprietary information.[62] Anonymous has since been involved in numerous incidents of data exposure to advance both political and social stances. In October 2011, Anonymous targeted online child pornography sites; after the Freedom Hosting server ignored Anonymous' warnings to remove links to illegal child pornography sites, the hacker collective infiltrated the server, took down over 40 child pornography websites, and exposed the names of nearly 1,600 active members of these sites.[63]

Some have even likened Anonymous to "the non-state insurgents the U.S. has faced in Iraq and Afghanistan—small groups of non-state actors using asymmetric means of warfare to destabilize and disrupt existing political authority."[64] Whereas traditional insurgencies may desire to weaken the control or legitimacy of an established government, some have suggested that the goals of the Anonymous "insurgents" may be slightly different. It has been posited that Anonymous actors— as insurgents—may desire independence from the government in the sense that government should not control the cyber domain.[65]

How groups like Anonymous are conceptualized may drive the policies and strategies adopted to address their actions. Is Anonymous a group of online activists, a collection of hacker criminals, or a cyber insurgency? And, because Anonymous is known to be a loosely connected organization, can all members and actors be assimilated into the same category? Members' differing goals and activities may require that a variety of conceptualizations be applied to Anonymous and that a range of strategies be employed to counter any illegal activities. In its counter-Anonymous activities to date, the U.S. government has primarily treated the collective as a criminal entity and has indicted and arrested individuals associated with specific hacking and data breach incidents.

- In March 2012, the Department of Justice indicted six individuals in the United States and abroad for hacking and other crimes related to their participation in

---

(...continued)

January 23, 2008.

[59] James Harrison, "Scientology Protestors Take Action Around World," *The State News*, February 12, 2008.

[60] E. Gabriella Coleman, "Anonymous: From the Lulz to Collective Action," *The New Everyday*, April 6, 2011.

[61] From remarks by Gabriella Coleman, Professor, New York University, at The Brookings Institution, *Hacktivism, Vigilantism and Collective Action in a Digital Age*, November 9, 2011.

[62] "HBGary Federal Hacked by Anonymous," *KrebsOnSecurity*, February 7, 2011.

[63] "Anonymous Targets Child Porn Sites, Releases Names of 1,500 Members," *Homeland Security News Wire*, October 25, 2011.

[64] Paul Rosenzweig, *Lessons of WikiLeaks: The U.S. Needs a Counterinsurgency Strategy for Cyberspace*, The Heritage Foundation, Backgrounder #2560, May 31, 2011, http://www.heritage.org/research/reports/2011/05/lessons-of-wikileaks-the-us-needs-a-counterinsurgency-strategy-for-cyberspace.

[65] Ibid.

Anonymous and related groups.[66] The indictment cites the December 2011 hacking of Stratfor and theft of confidential information of about 860,000 individuals. It also references the January 2012 hacking of international law enforcement email and subsequent accessing of a conference call between Ireland's national police, the FBI, and other law enforcement agencies.

- In July 2011, the FBI arrested 16 individuals for their alleged role in Anonymous' DDoS attack on PayPal. After WikiLeaks released the trove of State Department cables in November 2010, PayPal suspended WikiLeaks' account such that it could no longer receive donations via PayPal. This spurred "Operation Avenge Assange," where Anonymous coordinated DDoS attacks against PayPal's (and other companies') servers.[67]

Government Definitions and Agency Focus

The U.S. government does not appear to have an official definition of cybercrime that distinguishes it from crimes committed in what many consider the real world. Similarly, there is not a definition of cybercrime that distinguishes it from other forms of cyber threats, and the term is often used interchangeably with other Internet or technology-based malicious acts such as cyber warfare, cyber attack, and cyber terrorism.[68] Rather, government officials, law enforcement, and policymakers have often described cybercrime in terms of a number of computer, Internet, or advanced technology-related offenses. It has been an umbrella term, encompassing a range of crimes and malicious activities that may differ depending upon who is asked.

Federal law enforcement agencies often define cybercrime based on their jurisdiction and the crimes they are charged with investigating. And, just as there is no overarching definition for cybercrime, there is no single agency that has been designated as the lead investigative agency for combating "cybercrime." For instance, a range of federal law enforcement agencies, including the Federal Bureau of Investigation (FBI), U.S. Secret Service (Secret Service, USSS), and others, investigate crimes that have high-tech elements or that may be considered cybercrimes.

- The FBI is the primary investigative agency within DOJ charged with combating a variety of crimes that may be considered under the broader category of cybercrime. The FBI works cases ranging from computer hacking and online intellectual property rights violations to child exploitation via the Internet and a range of online frauds such as advance fee fraud (AFF), identity theft, and healthcare scams—all elements of what the FBI considers cybercrime.[69] The FBI has a Cyber Division that is involved in investigating these crimes as well as other cyber threats. However, because of the multi-faceted nature of many of these crimes, other divisions are likely involved in their investigation as well.

---

[66] These groups include Internet Feds, LulzSec, and AntiSec.

[67] U.S. Department of Justice, Federal Bureau of Investigation, "Sixteen Individuals Arrested in the United States for Alleged Roles in Cyber Attacks," press release, July 19, 2011, http://www.fbi.gov/news/pressrel/press-releases/sixteen-individuals-arrested-in-the-united-states-for-alleged-roles-in-cyber-attacks.

[68] McAfee provides examples of cybercrime, hacktivism, cyber war, and cyber terrorism at http://blogs mcafee.com/wp-content/uploads/2010/10/CybercrimeAndHactivismFocus2010.pdf.

[69] For more information on the full range of the FBI's cyber investigations, see http://www fbi.gov/about-us/investigate/cyber.

- The Internet Crime Complaint Center (IC3)—a partnership between the FBI and the National White Collar Crime Center[70] (NW3C)—views cybercrime as a term encompassing "online fraud in its many forms including Intellectual Property Rights (IPR) matters, Computer Intrusions (hacking), Economic Espionage (Theft of Trade Secrets), Online Extortion, International Money Laundering, Identity Theft, and a growing list of Internet facilitated crimes."[71]

- Within the Department of Homeland Security (DHS), the Secret Service is one of the primary agencies combating what may be considered cybercrime. The USSS does not, however, have a publicly available definition for what it considers cybercrime. The USSS is charged with protecting the nation's financial infrastructure and payment systems to safeguard the economy. As such, it has established a Cyber Intelligence Unit, 38 Financial Crimes Task Forces, and 31 Electronic Fraud Task Forces that investigate a range of crimes, including those with a cyber component.[72]

- The Council of Europe Convention on Cybercrime,[73] to which the United States is a signatory, defines cybercrime as a range of malicious activities that fall into four broad categories of computer-related crimes: (1) security breaches such as hacking, illegal data interception, and system interferences that compromise network integrity and availability; (2) fraud and forgery; (3) child pornography; and (4) copyright infringements. While the United States has signed the Convention, it has not necessarily adopted the exact definition of cybercrime as laid out in the Convention.[74]

In prosecuting cases with a cyber component, DOJ does not explicitly define cybercrime or comprehensively list all offenses that may be considered cybercrimes. Data on cybercrime prosecutions tend to reflect cases prosecuted under the computer fraud statute,[75] 18 U.S.C. §1030, as well as those statutes related to stored wire and electronic communications, 18 U.S.C. §2101-2711.[76] DOJ does indicate, however, that other cybercrimes are prosecuted under federal fraud, identity theft, illegal intercept of electronic communications, access device fraud, illegal access to

---

[70] The NW3C is supported by a grant from the Bureau of Justice Assistance. For more information on the Center, see http://www.nw3c.org/.

[71] Internet Crime Complaint Center, http://www.ic3.gov/about/default.aspx.

[72] Information provided to CRS by the USSS Office of Congressional Affairs, November 22, 2011.

[73] A copy of the Convention is available at http://conventions.coe.int/Treaty/EN/Treaties/html/185.htm.

[74] Legislation has been introduced in the 112th Congress (e.g., S. 1469) that would, among other things, require the Administration to submit an annual report on foreign cybercrime activities and their impact on the U.S. government, persons, and commerce. It would use the definition of cybercrime as outlined in the Council of Europe Convention on Cybercrime.

[75] The federal computer fraud and abuse statute protects computers in which there is a federal interest—federal computers, bank computers, and computers used in or affecting interstate and foreign commerce. It shields them from trespassing, threats, damage, espionage, and from being corruptly used as instruments of fraud. For more information, see CRS Report 97-1025, *Cybercrime: An Overview of the Federal Computer Fraud and Abuse Statute and Related Federal Criminal Laws*, by Charles Doyle.

[76] U.S. Department of Justice, *United States Attorneys' Annual Statistical Report, Fiscal Year 2010*, pp. 26-27, http://www.justice.gov/usao/reading_room/reports/asr2010/10statrpt.pdf. The FY2011 report does not contain specific information on cybercrime.

---

stored communications, copyright infringement, and counterfeit products/trademark infringement statutes.[77]

Is a Definition Needed?

Some may question whether it is necessary to have a clear definition of what constitutes cybercrime and what delineates it from other real world and cyber threats. And the answer may depend on the purpose of defining it.

On one hand, if the purpose of defining cybercrime is for investigating and prosecuting any of the various crimes under the broader cybercrime umbrella, it may be less critical to create a definition of the umbrella term and more imperative to clearly define which specific activities constitute crimes—regardless of whether they are considered real world crimes or cybercrimes. For instance, identity theft (18 U.S.C. §1028(a)(7)) is a crime whether it is committed solely in the real world or carried out via cyber means. The statute does not distinguish between the means by which the crime is carried out.

On the other hand, a distinction between cybercrime and other malicious activities may be beneficial for creating specific policies on combating the ever-expanding range of cyber threats. Indeed, some have argued that the prevention and remediation of cybercrime hinge on definitional clarity.[78] If government agencies and private sector businesses design strategies and missions around combating "cybercrime," it may be useful to communicate a clear definition of cybercrime to those individuals who may be involved in carrying out the strategies. For instance, if Congress receives an appropriations request for agency funds to combat cybercrime, policymakers may find it beneficial to understand what is meant by the term *cybercrime* as well as what activities would be implemented to combat the threat before deciding whether or not, as well as the extent to which, appropriations may be warranted. Similarly, if Congress chooses to conduct oversight on agencies' efforts to combat cybercrime, a consensus definition of cybercrime and its distinction from various cyber threats may aid in making a sound evaluation of cybercrime policies and strategies.[79]

If, for policy implications, Congress is interested in evaluating the extent or impact of cybercrime—or the countermeasures aimed at thwarting cyber criminals—a definition may be necessary. More information on the issues surrounding "Measuring and Tracking Cybercrime" is provided later in this report.

Strategies and Cybercrime

The United States does not have a national strategy exclusively focused on combating cybercrime. Rather, there are other, broader strategies that have cybercrime components. Policymakers may question whether there should be a distinct strategy for combating cybercrime

---

[77] Ibid, p. 27.

[78] Sarah Gordon and Richard Ford, "On the definition and classification of cybercrime," *Journal of Computer Virology*, vol. 2 (July 2006), p. 13.

[79] For example, the International Cybercrime Reporting and Cooperation Act (S. 1469) from the 112th Congress would define cybercrime as the range of criminal offenses outlined in the Council of Europe Convention of Cybercrime.

or whether efforts to control these crimes are best addressed through more wide-ranging strategies, such as those targeting cybersecurity or transnational organized crime. Congress may also question whether these broader strategies provide specific cybercrime-related objectives and clear means to achieve these goals.

The framework within which cybercrime is conceptualized may provide a backdrop for evaluating what type of strategy—existing or otherwise—may be best leveraged to counter the modern day cybercrime threats. For instance, if cybercrime is thought of more as a national security threat than a public security threat, a strategy focused on countering national security threats (including cyber threats) may be more appropriate than a public security-focused strategy for confronting cybercrime, and vice versa. However, categorically clumping the collection of cybercrime activities under the umbrella of "national security threat," "economic security threat," "public security threat," etc. may prove challenging because of the range of crimes and variety of malicious actors. As such, another means of examining what form of strategy to employ regarding cybercrime may be to take an "all threats" approach specific to the cyber domain. This type of strategy would focus on the cyber space (as opposed to the physical space) through which the criminal activity takes place, regardless of the security level of the threat.

Some have suggested that the starting point for any strategy addressing cybercrime should focus on actor attribution and that "greater attribution and clearer rules for responding to both non-attributed and attributed attacks would enable the development and implementation of better strategies and tactics for responding to cyber threats."[80] Existing methods for responding to attacks in the physical world differ based on the identity and motivation of the actor. For example, legal frameworks direct that law enforcement responds to criminal actors, the intelligence community engages in counterintelligence, and the military addresses threats posed by nation-states.[81] In the cyber world, however, these different actors may use similar techniques. As such, attributing a given incident to a particular individual or entity—and responding within the appropriate legal framework—may be challenging.

The **Appendix** presents a selection of current U.S. strategies and international conventions in which the United States participates. Policymakers may evaluate the effectiveness of these existing tools in enhancing actor attribution and countering the spectrum of evolving cybercrime threats. While any one given strategy may be insufficient to address the array of cybercrime threats, the interplay between several strategies may provide a framework for effective crime fighting in the digital domain. Congressional oversight may highlight any gaps in strategies and may be able to evaluate whether the strategies are designed (and carried out) to work with one another.

Measuring and Tracking Cybercrime

According to one expert, "the threat of cybercrime is largely being ignored, and that [threat] is greater than most people believe."[82] However, comprehensive data on cybercrime incidents and

---

[80] Scott Charney, *Rethinking the Cyber Threat: A Framework and Path Forward*, Trustworthy Computing Group, Microsoft Corporation, 2009, p. 12.

[81] Ibid., p. 6-7.

[82] "Attackers Have Advantage in Cyberspace, Says Cybersecurity Expert," *Homeland Security Newswire*, August 12, 2011, http://www.homelandsecuritynewswire.com/attackers-have-advantage-cyberspace-says-cybersecurity-expert.

their impact are not available, and without exact numbers on the current scope and prevalence of cybercrime, it is difficult to evaluate the magnitude of the threats posed by cyber criminals.

There are a number of issues that have prevented the accurate measurement and tracking of cybercrime. Firstly, the lack of a clear definition of what constitutes cybercrime presents a barrier to tracking comprehensive cybercrime data. This is compounded by the facts that (1) the range of cybercrimes is ever expanding in the globalized world and (2) cyber crimes often overlap with more traditional, non-cyber crimes—thus providing challenges in gauging the true scope of cybercrime. Various agencies and researchers have put forth estimates of the prevalence and costs of cybercrime. However, these often measure a different range of criminal activities and base estimates on differing victim populations.

- The Ponemon Institute, through its Second Annual Cost of Cyber Crime Study (2011), estimates that the median cost of cybercrime to select organizations is $5.9 million annually.[83] Further, the study's findings suggest that this median cost increased by 56% from $3.8 million to $5.9 million in 2010 and 2011, respectively. The median cost is based on a self-report survey of 50 U.S.-based organizations across various industry sectors. In its report, the Ponemon Institute did not provide a definition of cybercrime as used in the survey or report of the findings. Further, no information was provided on whether survey documents provided to the study participants included a definition of "cybercrime" that was to be used throughout the survey.

- Results from DOJ's National Computer Security Survey in 2005 indicate that the more than 7,800 businesses responding to the survey detected over 22 million incidents of cybercrime in 2005.[84] These incidents resulted in $867 million in losses. For purposes of the survey, DOJ considered cybercrime to encompass cyber attacks, cyber theft, and "other computer security incidents."[85] This survey tapped information from businesses only—not individuals—and as such, did not evaluate the prevalence of some cybercrimes, such as online pornography and cyberstalking, that may more likely impact individuals than corporations.

Some surveys of cybercrime measure a specific aspect of what may be considered cybercrime, such as phishing attempts or data breaches. Indeed, the prevalence of data breaches is an often-cited statistic, related to an unknown—and by no means comprehensive—range of cybercrimes. The number of data breaches, as well as the number of records affected by these breaches, has fluctuated over the past several years.

---

[83] Ponemon Institute, *Second Annual Cost of Cyber Crime Study, Benchmark Study of U.S. Companies*, August 2011, p. 1, http://www.arcsight.com/collateral/whitepapers/2011_Cost_of_Cyber_Crime_Study_August.pdf. This is based on a sample of 50 companies with over 700 employees. Annual losses ranged from $1.5 million to $36.5 million per organization.

[84] Ramona R. Rantala, *Cybercrime Against Businesses, 2005*, Bureau of Justice Statistics, U.S. Department of Justice, NCJ221943, September 2008, http://bjs.ojp.usdoj.gov/content/pub/pdf/cb05.pdf.

[85] Cyber attacks were defined as "crimes in which the computer system is the target. Cyber attacks consist of computer viruses (including worms and Trojan horses), denial of service attacks, and electronic vandalism or sabotage." Cyber theft was considered to encompass "crimes in which a computer is used to steal money or other things of value. Cyber theft includes embezzlement, fraud, theft of intellectual property, and theft of personal or financial data." Other computer security incidents included "spyware, adware, hacking, phishing, spoofing, pinging, port scanning, and theft of other information, regardless of whether the breach was successful or damage or losses were sustained as a result." Ibid., p.2.

- The Identity Theft Resource Center (ITRC) tracks data breaches across the nation, and their statistics indicate that the total number of reported data breaches decreased in 2011 (n = 419) after steadily increasing between 2005 and 2008 (n = 656), dipping in 2009 (n = 498), and then increasing again in 2010 (n = 662).[86]

- Symantec observed the prevalence of malicious Internet activity—including malicious code, spam zombies, phishing hosts, and bots—across the globe.[87] The United States ranked at the top of the list, having 19% of the malicious activity, followed by China (8%) and Brazil (6%).[88] While this report includes data on a range of malicious Internet activities, it does not provide information as to the prevalence of all forms of cybercrime around the world.

Self-Reporting Cybercrime Victimization

One noteworthy factor impacting availability of data on cybercrime prevalence and its impact is that much of the available data on cybercrime is self-reported. Some have speculated that this self-reporting leads to an underestimation of the true breadth and impact of victimization. This underestimation may be due in part to victims' lack of knowledge that a specific crime has occurred (and its subsequent impact). This underestimation of the scope of cybercrime may also be due to victims' unwillingness to report a crime. For instance, "[m]any financial organisations still prefer to draw a veil over the issue of cybercrime losses because of the technological 'lack' it suggests in their operations."[89] Companies may fear that reporting data breaches could damage their professional reputations and lead to customers/consumers pulling their support and patronage. Individuals may also be unlikely to report such crime if they view their subsequent losses as relatively small and not worth their time and money to report to officials.

Others, however, have suggested that self-report surveys may lead to an overestimation of the prevalence or magnitude of the cybercrime threat. This could be in part because errors in estimated losses—in terms of the amount of data or number of dollars lost to cybercrime—are always positive; there are no negative loss estimation errors because individuals do not report negative losses from cybercrime. Outliers in estimated cybercrime losses may impact survey results and drive up the findings on estimated losses. As such, any average errors in estimated losses may be skewed to have an upward bias.[90]

---

[86] See CRS Report R40599, *Identity Theft: Trends and Issues*, by Kristin M. Finklea, Identity Theft Resource Center, http://www.idtheftcenter.org/artman2/publish/lib_survey/ITRC_2008_Breach_List.shtml. The IRTC indicates that the criteria for qualifying as a data breach is "[a]ny name or number that may be used, alone or in conjunction with other information, to identify a specific individual, including: name, social security number, date of birth. Banking or financial account number, credit card or debit card number with or without a PIN, official state or government issued driver's license or identification number, passport identification number, alien registration number, employer or taxpayer identification number, or insurance policy or subscriber numbers; unique biometric data; [or] electronic identification number, address or routing code or telecommunication identifying information or device."

[87] It gathered this information from over "240,000 sensors in over 200 countries and territories [that] monitor attack activity through a combination of Symantec products and services...." Symantec, *Symantec Internet Security Threat Report: Trends for 2009*, Volume XV, April 2010, p6, http://eval.symantec.com/mktginfo/enterprise/white_papers/b-whitepaper_exec_summary_internet_security_threat_report_xv_04-2010.en-us.pdf

[88] For more information on the top 10 countries impacted by malicious Internet activity, see Ibid., p. 7.

[89] John E Dunn, TechWorld, "Cybercrime Now Major Drag on Financial Services, PwC Finds," *NetworkWorld*, March 27, 2012.

[90] Dinei Florêncio and Cormac Herley, "The Cybercrime Wave That Wasn't," *The New York Times*, April 14, 2012.

Another factor that may contribute to unreliable self-reported victimization data is that individuals may be reporting victimization to one or more types of entities—or not at all. For instance, while some victims may file a report with consumer protection entities such as the Internet Crime Complaint Center or the Federal Trade Commission's Consumer Sentinel database, others may file complaints with credit bureaus, while still others may file complaints with law enforcement. Not all victims, however, may file complaints with consumer protection entities, credit reporting agencies, and law enforcement. This uneven reporting can thus distort overall estimates of victimization.

Rather than measuring the cybercrime problem solely in terms of estimated victim losses, researchers have raised the idea of measuring the extent of the cybercrime problem as a ratio of cybercrime consumer losses to cybercrime perpetrator profits. One researcher has noted that

> [t]he harm experienced by users [consumers] rather than the (much smaller) gain achieved by hackers is the true measure of the cybercrime problem. Surveys that perpetuate the myth that cybercrime makes for easy money are harmful because they encourage hopeful, if misinformed, new entrants, who generate more harm for users than profit for themselves.[91]

Moving Forward

Policymakers may debate whether to direct an evaluation of the threats posed by cybercriminals. A comprehensive study could include an appraisal of costs to U.S. persons and businesses alike. Some may argue that any such study should necessarily include well-delineated parameters for what constitutes cybercrime—whether defined by policymakers, a law enforcement community, or cyber scholars.

With a clear assessment of the breadth of the cybercrime threat, policymakers may be positioned to assess whether federal law enforcement has the tools and resources—both funding and manpower—to combat these threats. Congress has often examined cybercrime and related federal resources in the broader context of ensuring cybersecurity. And, policymakers have expressed interest in ensuring the strength and efficacy of the federal cyber workforce. As such, understanding the true nature and scope of the cyber threat may help Congress conduct oversight in these areas and ensure that the relevant resources are appropriately positioned.

---

[91] Ibid.

Appendix. Existing Strategies and Cybercrime

This appendix presents a selection of current U.S. strategies and international conventions in which the United States participates. While these strategies do not all directly address cybercrime, many address a broad array of cyber threats or criminal threats under which cybercrime may be considered. Of note, the strategies presented below are organized by date of release or U.S. adoption.

Department of Defense Strategy for Operating in Cyberspace

In July 2011 the Office of the Secretary of Defense issued a document called the *Department of Defense Strategy for Operating in Cyberspace*, also known as the Five Strategic Initiatives.[92] This strategy does not specifically target cybercrime threats—though it notes that "[t]he tools and techniques developed by cyber criminals are increasing in sophistication at an incredible rate"[93]— and instead addresses cyber security on the whole. Its first initiative reiterates the Department of Defense's (DOD's) position that cyberspace is an operational domain to organize, train, and equip in order to take full advantage of its potential. The second initiative is to employ new defense operating concepts to protect DOD networks and systems, while the third is to partner with other departments, agencies, and the private sector to enable a whole-of-government cyber security strategy. The fourth initiative focuses on relationship building with U.S. allies and international partners, and the fifth intends to leverage the U.S. cyber workforce and technological innovation.

Although usually directed at military targets, not all intrusions on DOD networks are the result of a combatant. The Defense Cyber Crime Center (DC3) is a forensics, research, and training organization to assist with criminal investigations of network security breaches on DOD networks and cyber intrusions presenting a national security threat.[94] The DC3 is also responsible for the Defense Industrial Base Collective Information Sharing Environment (DCISE), a clearinghouse for threat data between DOD and its industry partners.

Strategy to Combat Transnational Organized Crime

In July 2011, the Obama Administration released the *Strategy to Combat Transnational Organized Crime: Addressing Converging Threats to National Security*.[95] The strategy provides the federal government's first broad conceptualization of "transnational organized crime," highlighting it as a national security concern.[96] It highlights 10 primary threat categories posed by transnational organized crime: penetration of state institutions, corruption, and threats to governance; threats to the economy, U.S. competitiveness, and strategic markets; nexus between

---

[92] U.S. Department of Defense, *Department of Defense Strategy for Operating in Cyberspace*, July 2011, http://www.defense.gov/news/d20110714cyber.pdf.

[93] Ibid., p. 3.

[94] For more information on the DC3, see http://www.dc3.mil.

[95] The White House, *Strategy To Combat Transnational Organized Crime: Addressing Converging Threats to National Security*, July 2011, http://www.whitehouse.gov/sites/default/files/microsites/2011-strategy-combat-transnational-organized-crime.pdf. (Hereafter *Strategy To Combat Transnational Organized Crime*.)

[96] For a discussion of organized crime and this strategy, see CRS Report R41547, *Organized Crime: An Evolving Challenge for U.S. Law Enforcement*, by Jerome P. Bjelopera and Kristin M. Finklea.

criminals, terrorists, and insurgents; expansion of drug trafficking; human smuggling; trafficking in persons; weapons trafficking; intellectual property theft; the critical role of facilitators;[97] and cybercrime. The strategy outlines six key priority actions to counter the range of threats posed by transnational organized crime:

- taking shared responsibility and identifying what actions the United States can take to protect against the threat and impact of transnational organized crime;

- enhancing intelligence and information sharing;

- protecting the financial system and strategic markets;

- strengthening interdiction, investigations, and prosecutions;

- disrupting drug trafficking and its facilitation of other transnational threats; and

- building international capacity, cooperation, and partnerships.[98]

While this strategy does not focus solely on cybercrime activities of criminal networks, it does include a prominent discussion surrounding organized crime's involvement in cybercrime. The strategy notes that "[v]irtually every transnational criminal organization and its enterprises are connected and enabled by information systems technologies, making cybercrime a substantially more important concern."[99] It also points out a significant impediment to law enforcement successfully investigating cybercriminal activities: "Crimes can occur more quickly, but investigations proceed more slowly due to the critical shortage of investigators with the knowledge and expertise to analyze ever increasing amounts of potential digital evidence."[100]

Further, a number of the threats identified in the strategy—while not specifically identified under the cybercrime umbrella—may overlap with cybercrime or may be directly facilitated by the Internet and other advanced technologies. For instance, the theft of intellectual property is often carried out through illegal computer intrusions and the digital extraction of information and thus could also be considered cybercrime. Indeed, many crimes or malicious activities can fall under various threat categories outlined by the strategy; for instance, many crimes related to financial fraud and identity theft may fall under the categories of cybercrime, intellectual property theft, or threats to the economy, U.S. competitiveness, and strategic markets. As such, this strategy does not provide a detailed outline for how the U.S. should counter each category of threat, and the Administration indicated that this strategy is meant to complement a range of other strategies, including the International Strategy for Cyberspace.[101]

International Strategy for Cyberspace

In May 2011, the Obama Administration issued the *International Strategy for Cyberspace: Prosperity, Security, and Openness in a Networked World*. This strategy outlines U.S. engagement

---

[97] "Facilitators" are "semi-legitimate players such as accountants, attorneys, notaries, bankers, and real estate brokers, who cross both the licit and illicit worlds and provide services to legitimate customers, criminals, and terrorists alike." See *Strategy To Combat Transnational Organized Crime*, p. 8.

[98] Ibid., p.4.

[99] Ibid., p. 3.

[100] Ibid., p. 8.

[101] Ibid., p. 4.

with international partners to confront the full array of cyber issues—including cybercrime.[102] According to this strategy, the U.S. Government's core principles are fundamental freedoms, privacy, and the free flow of information while protecting the security of national networks. Rather than imposing a global governance structure, the strategy recommends building international norms of behavior and enhancing interoperability.

The strategy outlines five principles that nations should support, one of which is protection from crime. Under this principle, nations are expected to "identify and prosecute cybercriminals, to ensure laws and practices deny criminals safe havens, and cooperate with international criminal investigations in a timely manner."[103] The strategy also provides a core set of seven policy priorities as well as proposed actions to accomplish each of these priorities. Directly relating to the prevention, investigation, and prosecution of cybercrime, one overarching policy priority involves extending law enforcement collaboration and rule of law. To accomplish this, the strategy proposes that the United States will

- fully participate in the development of international cybercrime policy,

- encourage nations' participation in the Council of Europe Convention on Cybercrime,

- direct cybercrime legislation toward combating illegal activities rather than restricting Internet access, and

- prevent Internet exploitation by terrorists and criminals seeking to plan, finance, or carry out malicious activities.[104]

The International Strategy for Cyberspace addresses cybercrime in the broader context of cyber security. Moreover, it primarily discuses how the United States will increase its domestic and multilateral cybercrime fighting capacities.

National Strategy for Trusted Identities in Cyberspace

The Obama Administration released the *National Strategy for Trusted Identities in Cyberspace: Enhancing Online Choice, Efficiency, Security, and Privacy* in April 2011. In this strategy, the Administration proposed an "Identity Ecosystem" where individuals and organizations adhere to standards to authenticate their online identities and the identities of their digital devices. It was suggested that this ecosystem would provide, among other things, enhanced security such that it would be more difficult for criminals to compromise online transactions.[105] Further, the strategy posits that an environment with secure authentication can support forensics to "maximize recovery efforts, enable enhancements to protect against evolving threats, and permit attribution, when appropriate, to ensure that criminals can be held accountable for their activities."[106] In

---

[102] The White House, *International Strategy for Cyberspace: Prosperity, Security, and Openness in a Networked World*, May 2011, http://www.whitehouse.gov/sites/default/files/rss_viewer/internationalstrategy_cyberspace.pdf.

[103] Ibid., p. 10. The other four principles to which nations should adhere include upholding fundamental freedoms, respecting property, valuing privacy, and retaining the right to self-defense.

[104] Ibid., pp. 19-20.

[105] The White House, *National Strategy for Trusted Identities in Cyberspace: Enhancing Online Choice, Efficiency, Security, and Privacy*, April 2011, http://www.whitehouse.gov/sites/default/files/rss_viewer/NSTICstrategy_041511.pdf.

[106] Ibid., p. 12-13.

---

encouraging major vendors and companies to take up enhanced standards for verifying user identities and storing personal data online, this strategy provides one step in protecting information online.[107]

Council of Europe Convention on Cybercrime

The Council of Europe's Convention on Cybercrime was developed in 2001 to address several categories of crimes committed via the Internet and other information networks.[108] It is the first—and only[109]—international treaty on this issue, and its primary goal is to "pursue a common criminal policy aimed at the protection of society against cybercrime, especially by adopting appropriate legislation and fostering international co-operation." To date, 47 countries are signatories to the convention and 31 of these—including the United States—have ratified it.[110]

Signatories to the convention must define criminal offenses and sanctions under their domestic laws for four categories of computer-related crimes: (1) security breaches such as hacking, illegal data interception, and system interferences that compromise network integrity and availability; (2) fraud and forgery; (3) child pornography; and (4) copyright infringements. The convention also requires signatories to establish domestic procedures for detecting, investigating, and prosecuting computer crimes, as well as collecting electronic evidence of any criminal offense. It also requires that signatories engage in international cooperation "to the widest extent possible."

There has been a debate about whether there should be a global standard—be it the Convention or a different entity—for dealing with cybercrime.[111] Some have suggested that a global convention could help countries harmonize their legislation on cybercrime. One argument in this case is that similar legislation across countries could enhance international cooperation since a number of countries base mutual legal assistance on the notion of "dual criminality," wherein an action that is illegal in one country is also considered a crime in the other.[112] Others, however, have expressed reservations about supporting a global standard for combating cybercrime. Concerns have centered not only around the feasibility of global coordination, but around whether such legal harmonization could put certain nations in a position of enforcing laws that may depart from the nation's basic tenets;[113] for instance, could laws curbing certain levels of inflammatory "speech" online infringe upon the right to free speech guaranteed in the United States, and if so, how would the United States balance enforcing harmonized global laws with ensuring constitutional rights?

---

[107] Nicole Perlroth, "Even Big Companies Cannot Protect Their Data," *The New York Times*, January 17, 2012.

[108] For more information on the Convention, see archived CRS Report RS21208, *Cybercrime: The Council of Europe Convention*, by Kristin Archick. A copy of the Convention is available at http://conventions.coe.int/Treaty/EN/Treaties/html/185.htm.

[109] Duncan B. Hollis, "An e-SOS for Cyberspace," *Harvard International Law Journal*, vol. 52 (2011), pp. 392-393.

[110] The U.S. Senate ratified the Convention on August 3, 2006. For the current list of signatories and ratifications, see http://conventions.coe.int/Treaty/Commun/ChercheSig.asp?NT=185&CM=1&DF=&CL=ENG.

[111] Brian Harley, "A Global Convention on Cybercrime?," *The Columbia Science and Technology Law Review*, March 23, 2010, http://www.stlr.org/2010/03/a-global-convention-on-cybercrime/.

[112] See, for example, Twelfth United Nations Congress on Crime Prevention and Criminal Justice, *Recent Developments in the Use of Science and Technology by Offenders and by Competent Authorities in Fighting Crime, Including the Case of Cybercrime*, United Nations, Working paper prepared by the Secretariat, January 22, 2010.

[113] Brian Harley, "A Global Convention on Cybercrime?," *The Columbia Science and Technology Law Review*, March 23, 2010, http://www.stlr.org/2010/03/a-global-convention-on-cybercrime/.

Global Internet Freedom

In 2006, the Department of State launched the Global Internet Freedom Task Force (GIFT). The GIFT's main foreign policy objective is enhancing global Internet freedom by monitoring human rights abuses and enhancing access to the Internet through technical and financial support for increasing availability in the developing world. A form of expanding access to the Internet is to create mirror sites that serve as alternatives to websites that are blocked in some countries, or to develop tools and instructions that enable users to work around a country's firewalls. The International Strategy for Cyberspace and Global Internet Freedom initiatives present a very different view of cyberspace from DOD doctrine, which emphasizes full spectrum dominance and cyberspace as an operational, war-fighting domain.

A question exists about the definition of sovereignty in cyberspace. Although no one country "owns" cyberspace, each may have the authority to regulate its portion of the Internet, similar to territorial waters or airspace. What constitutes computer-based crime may be determined by domestic standards, and one country's Internet freedom initiative may be another country's cybercrime.

National Strategy to Secure Cyberspace

Following the terrorist attacks of September 11, 2001, the newly formed Department of Homeland Security (DHS) issued a document that recognized cyberspace as a strategic asset with national security implications and offered suggestions for private network owners and operators to increase protection efforts. The 2003 *National Strategy to Secure Cyberspace* places DHS as the lead for coordinating federal network protection as well as working with the private sector, and also offers a framework for improving international cooperation. The strategy prioritizes five components to securing cyberspace:

- a national cyberspace security response system,

- a national cyberspace security threat and vulnerability reduction program,

- a national cyberspace security awareness and training program,

- securing governments' cyberspace, and

- national security and international cyberspace security cooperation.[114]

Like the *International Strategy for Cyberspace*, the *National Strategy to Secure Cyberspace* addresses cybercrime in the broader context of cyber security. Within this context, it prioritizes improving U.S. response to cyber incidents and reducing any potential damage, reducing threats from and vulnerabilities to cyber attacks—including cybercrime—and preventing cyber attacks.

---

[114] U.S. Department of Homeland Security, *The National Strategy to Secure Cyberspace*, February 2003, p. x, http://www.us-cert.gov/reading_room/cyberspace_strategy.pdf.

Author Contact Information

Kristin M. Finklea
Specialist in Domestic Security
kfinklea@crs.loc.gov, 7-6259

Catherine A. Theohary
Analyst in National Security Policy and Information
Operations
ctheohary@crs.loc.gov, 7-0844